TOWARD

TOWARD

Poems

Moira Linehan

SLANT

TOWARD
Poems

Slant
An Imprint of Wipf and Stock Publishers
199 W. 8th Ave., Suite 3
Eugene, OR 97401

www.wipfandstock.com

HARDCOVER ISBN: 978-1-7252-5280-6
PAPERBACK ISBN: 978-1-7252-5279-0
EBOOK ISBN: 978-1-7252-5281-3

Cataloguing-in-Publication data:

Names: Linehan, Moira.

Title: Toward : poems / Moira Linehan.

Description: Eugene, OR: Slant, 2020.

Identifiers: ISBN 978-1-7252-5280-6 (hardcover) | ISBN 978-1-7252-5279-0 (paperback) | ISBN 978-1-7252-5281-3 (ebook)

Subjects: LCSH: American poetry -- 21st century | Irish Americans -- Poetry | Nature -- Poetry | Religious poetry, American.

Classification: PS3612.I538 T69 2020 (print) | PS3612.I538 (ebook)

Manufactured in the U.S.A.   MAY 12, 2020

Once again, in memory of Daniel Ounjian

and for Renata and David
and Daniel, Matthew, and Evan

CONTENTS

ONE

WHERE THERE'S A HISTORY OF FAMINE

They're always eating the grass.
One or two look up, startled, when I walk near.
They go on chewing.
Four o'clock one afternoon I hear a herder whistle.
His sheep come panting.
What does he have that they want?

Locals said it was coming,
the hurricane off Bermuda, turned this way.
All week winds had moaned.
Now screeching, they huddle round the cauldron of this cottage.
Through the night they howl.
The surf's pounding's drowned out.

Next day, the winds come off the cliffs.
They swell the waves, march them toward the West Cork hills.
The waves spume white froth.
Heavy, black-brimmed clouds follow after in endless parade.
I climb toward land's end.
Winds won't let me walk straight.

The sky's clearing. I chance it.
I've not yet walked down to the abbey's ruins.
Crows raise a ruckus,
flush a feather-thin pheasant with its hurrying trail of tail.
Only the well-fed
could find meat on those bones.

A famine's reach—like this land.
Where the heavens lower their weight on dark clouds.
The bay and rain blur.
The horizon, a vast front for thousands of miles of sea.
Where those left built cairns
at the backs of their mouths.

SPIRIT SEEKING

That which each being lacks is infinite.
—PAUL CLAUDEL

The fingers of the bay's containment, stone-bound land
thrust out into a sea with no other boundaries
in sight, that sea's pounding blows, only whispers
of what roils below under a sky that can
threaten to drop torrents, then return with birdsong
after a night of bone-harrowing gales. The first

who journeyed to this edge had searched for such a place.
No, that was much later. First, before even coming
together—how ever many of them there were—before
saying one word, there was a wanting. Yet before
even putting that into words—see how far back
this goes?—there was a need. And that's what's driven me

to return to these desolate cliffs rising above
an ever-shifting bay. Led by the force of their need,
those who first hallowed this place of mist and stone
and wind heard the rocks themselves cry out. There's never
silence. I'm with them, they with me in the spirit here
which can neither be created nor destroyed.

ENTERING THE CILL RIALAIG LANDSCAPE

                    where cliffs face a bay
bathed in perpetual grave gray. Even on days
with sun, rain clouds are always on the way. Always
waves—racing in—fail to contain themselves. The weight
of the North Atlantic presses them, gales of wind
push them to break against the base of the cliffs.
But waves can't be destroyed so they're raised as spray
and raging foam. Way out on the wavering horizon,
fog fades to mist, mist pales to water-filled rays
of light, traces of the last storm's passage, the coming
grace of sun. All the while, two men in a lone bobbing boat
wait for fish in the midst of the bay. Sheep and cows
graze along the tops of the cliffs. Wind rakes the ferns.

                              *

Isn't it the sweep of it? Why I keep turning to keep
it all in my head, the eternally-seething sea
between these cliffs of grieving wet stone and the distant,
light-streaked line underneath the enormous domed clouds,
clouds that allow brief moments of sun and then release
sheets of rain. Mist and fog in the sweep west to east,
erasing the far hills and islands. Look again,
they're re-emerging while the sea's suspended
in each wave as it breathes in, gathers, and heaves itself
against the cliffs, erupting like fireworks into mist.
And that's if there's only a breeze. When the wind picks up,
it can beat so wildly I can't even think. Yet sheep
go on eating grass and weeds amidst their stone
enclosures. I can see an oratory's ruins
above me, an abbey's below. I'm so small here
I could evaporate into the weep of rain.

*

Yes, it's how wide the sky is, how high it rises,
the far horizon dividing earth from air, fine line
at times shining white light, at times impossible
to define as rain clouds and rain and fog lie on top.
High tide or low, there's never silence. Wild waves
of wind, wild waves of sea hike themselves up
the cliffs' sides. Magpies find and fly the thermals.
This site the pious sought. Their rocks remain:
beehive huts, the outline of an oratory,
inscribed stones still standing. Inside my cottage,
the upper back wall's a skylight facing the side
of the hillock. Birds fly in and out its rock clefts.
A cow with lichen-colored haunches pauses
on the high ridge. Here's where I've come to write.

*

Oh, so much rain over the row of desolate
stone cottages along the narrow road oh, so
close to the cliffs' edge. The harrowing possible
holds me back. Late October. The locals repeat,
Winter's approaching. The long loneliness
of cold, low clouds, blowing gales, evening's slow spread
of shadows by three o'clock. Look, I chose to return,
knowing it's not the cliffs' edge I should fear. It's isolation
no one survives. But I believe no soul does
without some. That's the narrow road I walk.
Off to the west, polar air collides with the warm
Gulf Stream, so rain without end. But also rainbows
with huge, distinct arches. Each of the three
I've seen has had an echo, so double rainbows.

*

The *X* on the new legend outside the ruins
of the abbey documents *Anseo Atá Tú,*
You Are Here at the entrance into the sacred
universe of ancient monks. Verses of psalms,
their music against a backdrop of winds that fuel
the fuming sea here at a bay's brutal edge.
A rain-filled seemingly useless life, ritual
of manual labor, day after day clearing rocks
and roots in pursuit of the most elemental.
Pared-down plainchant, conduit to the beyond.
Or tribute to these numinous surroundings.
For here, even rain can be translucent as the few,
far shafts falling way out on the horizon now.
This enclosure, a place they were not to leave,
place of extreme beauty where their Rule set them
on a perpetual journey. *X.* I am here
at a measureless entrance in union with them.

FRAYING BLUE ROPE

holds closed the wire fencing penning sheep in.
Bold blue or red painted swaths around their necks
or along their backsides say who's whose.

The slow-setting sun, sinking behind Bólus Head,
is now claiming the whole expanse of sky—
well, at least as far as West Cork—suffusing it

with its own peach-rose hues. Even the bay—
all day its gray creased by a light breeze—remains
fixed in place by the cliffs' massive fingers.

Rock walls quilt a patchwork of greens between
those cliffs and the rise of hills. When he left Cork—
as plunging a descent as would be a drop

from the cliffs here—my great grandfather carried
imprints of such vast containment in his genes.
Now on whatever cliff I find myself,

a part of him holds me there, if only
by fraying blue rope. Though even at that,
much closer to string than rope.

FROM THIS DISTANCE

Tyrone Guthrie Centre, County Monaghan

Rows a tractor cut into the hillside
across the lake. From this distance: ridges
of ribbing, the first rows of an afghan.
Or—shadows in the furrows—a washboard.

From this distance across the lake: ridges
cut into grassland too soggy to seed.
A furrowed washboard of shadows. Ghost lines.
Ditches where the Famine dead lay, grass-stained mouths.

Bogland too soggy to seed, famine or not.
Such hunger's cycled back and back through this land.
In the ditches, the dead with grass-stained mouths
while some shipped oats and corn to England.

A hunger's cycled back and back through my life:
family dead on family dead, in grief gnawed to bone.
While some shipped corn and oats to England,
how did my father's grandfather survive?

Famine's bones—my family's buried stories—
eat at the lines I can, and cannot, write.
How could my great grandfather have survived?
What's the hunger that now lives on in me?

Surrounding the lines I do, and do not, write:
ribbing, first rows of what may, or may not, comfort.
The history of a hunger. From a distance,
rows a tractor cut into a hillside.

GENEALOGY

In memory of Honora Buckley Linehan

July 19th, 1860,
the census for Easton, Massachusetts.
The fourth child of Daniel and Catherine Buckley,
Honora—my grandmother—appears,
a month old. Add four boarders—John Haydan,
Dan Rierdon, Pat Connell, Ed Sweeney. All
born in Ireland. All in their twenties. *Labourers*
says the record. Honora's father, too.
On that same day in the dwelling next door—
three families, thirteen names, the youngest
John Linehan, new-born son of Margaret and James.

1870. The Buckleys still have four boarders,
though the names have changed and they're much younger.
There's more detail of their work: *works on hinges*
this census says of Honora's father.
Works on railroad, of three of the boarders
while the fourth one *farms*. Home for Honora,
where so many would come and go. Imagine
the stories of longing she's hearing, all
in a language with no word for *emigrate*. *Exile*,
the closest they have. Each night at dinner,
Honora coming through that swinging door,
carrying bowls of potatoes boiled with cabbage
out from the kitchen into those stories
about the land they'd left, the mothers.

1880. Now Honora's father *sells milk.*
Eleven boarders work in the shovel shop,
the stories, now multiplied threefold.
Now the Linehans own the place next door.
James and his oldest, John, *work in the hinge shop.*
I know what I want next and there it is
in the state archives: July 7th, 1885—
Honora marries John, the boy next door,
which is where I wish this story could pause
so my grandmother could speak, say what home meant
when hers stood next door for the rest of her life
while inside she carried twenty-five years
of exile, the longing of who knows how many
for the ones they'd never see again.
After hearing those stories, what mother
would ever let go of her child? Or worse,
ever let her child get too close?

1910: *Number of children born this mother:*
10. Number of children living: 8. My father,
now a name on the census, my father
who grew up her youngest, though not her last.
She died the summer before I was born.
But hadn't I been there all along,
for what story ever starts fresh and clean?
Straight and clear the path through the archives
back to Honora. And back to those boarders,
the stories that exiled her, as she'd tell them
again and again in the ways she did,
and did not, hold my father. He held me.

NO ROAD

If you can call it such, in this instance
road, what winds along the cliffs, relative
term for walkers, not to mention cars. More a trail
slung between the steep rise and swollen sea
below. Where there's a widening, just back
from the edge: remains of five pre-Famine
dwellings, wet-brown rock walls left open
to storm-heavy skies, even the thickest thatch
roof long ago blown off. In one, flat rocks
wall up its doorway, its narrow window.
The dying dragged in stones, sealed their hovels tombs.

Wakes, large and loud, in my aunt's darkened home. When
was it I see myself, so very small, wandering
dimly-lit parlor to sitting room, sun room, dining?
My grandfather, great Uncle Dan, one of the many
others in my father's large family—who's in the open
casket in my Aunt Mary's living room? Front staircase
and back, I go up, I come down. I stay away
but still I overhear stories, all beginning
Remember.

An ocean away, I pass stone remains,
no map to the history within. No road.

WITNESS

Through heavy, metal-colored clouds: three shafts
of iridescent light, two streaming down toward
either end of the island shaped like a beached whale

in the midst of the bay and the third, a dazzle
over its wet back. A Triune God's long arms
pointing, *Here, here, here,* but also taking me in

as I'm paused in my climb along the cliffs,
just looking out at an overflow from rain.
Unbidden watery rays like the maddening,

scumbling way of grace. How walking toward the end
of wherever, I sometimes turn to look back, look out
and there it goes before my eyes—mist into air.

TOWARD

Tyrone Guthrie Centre, County Monaghan

I walk a mile down the road to Newbliss,
walk a mile away, walk the wooded path
along the lake and out onto the lane
winding between muddy green hills. I'm nowhere
but among mournful cows, their eyes bottomless
wells that know a soul's dark nights. All their lives
cows stay put. One foot to the next I keep
moving, an end point always in mind: village,
next hillock, rounding the lake's loop. On I walk
without being able to say why I must.
The language here has been lost, words like woods
cut down, hauled off, or abandoned. Yet
something remains of those who spoke it. What
has always been beyond words, even when
they had their own. That's where I'm headed.

TWO

ECHOGRAM

Friday Harbor, WA

To those who are not ashamed of economy

     and right away there's that echo of you, my Love

Mrs. Child dedicating her book to housewives

     word meaning "the art of managing a household"

The American Frugal Housewife, 1833

     that meaning no longer used but bringing you to me

already a twelfth edition, the one I found

     for I hear "economics," picture you before a class

recipes, remedies, no nonsense advice

     pie charts and graphs for the flow of money through banks

for gathering fragments of time and materials

     you, my depth finder, now finding me at this harbor

all the string and brown paper, scraps of yarn, rags

     echogram in hand to show you're still taking note

even rags can be cut to strips, braided into mats

     no matter the distance or direction I've come, you've gone.

TOO MUCH TO TAKE IN

The long pulpy fibers of scrolls
absorb dyes unevenly.

—Exhibition notes

Now it's Chicago I explore
without you. Home for a month—this

cavernous room, view of brick backs
of old buildings, newer high rises

in the distance, reflecting glass.
Will I ever write a poem

where grief doesn't surface? Twelve stories
below, at intersections, shaded

canyons stretch between skyscrapers.
To show this woman hunched over

a blank page, I'd use very little
ink, just the tip of a dry brush.

WIDOW'S WALKS

They had to have climbed—the wives of sea captains, ships'
first mates and on down the line, the wives, the betrothed
of harpooners and deck hands, climbed belfries above
where they worshiped, climbed to the roofs where they lived, up
dark narrow stairways, steep ladder-like steps, ladders
themselves, ascending, holding on to railings or rungs,
rope lines or walls, heading straight up by the chimney
or winding around the tower, each the need to see
for herself, my need now, up Nantucket's First
Congregational Tower, how much closer to him
could she get, I get, than this horizon so vast,
so empty, that glorious many-masted vessel
long gone. Not returning. *No, not widow's walks,*
says the church member I meet at the top. *Just walks,*
those white-railed platforms around or next to a home's
central chimney, where they checked for the build-up of pitch,
pine the wood they burned, kept burning, where they stored buckets
of sand to throw on fires started so easily.
Likewise, the librarian insists *walks, not widow's*
walks. Okay, not widow's walks, romantic term
a journalist coined decades later. But I say
they had to have climbed. Right there in front of them
and all that longing to look beyond, long her refusal
to believe he would not return, longer yet

her longing for him, how it rolls in and over
without warning, like fog, then the inevitable
climb back down, the pitching forward, having to hold
myself back, hands out to hold onto anything,
still descending down, down, when does it end—that walk?

SENTENCE

The lost time of his life, a street fifteen years long,
but at least going somewhere, crisscrossing south, north,
back again and then at last, to Mississippi.
One long list of states, the street Faulkner's Joe Christmas
wandered. Those fifteen years in one sentence, midpoint
in the novel, lust mentioned, but just one sentence,
no room for lust's details. The words' luster dazzles,
propels me forward though not as I've lived my one
long sentence of grief, fifteen years and then some. Oh,
I should not have said *sentence*. One word's more like it:
listless. Everlastingly so. I'm still at a loss
to say where in grief I am. Ministering so long
to my lost, late love, crisscrossing north, south, and back,
I'm with him. I'm without. I meander in place.

THE SCULPTOR AND HIS MUSE

Auguste Rodin, 1894

She stands on one foot on his lap, balanced
by one hand there too, her other leg and arm
stretched out straight behind, that hand holding up
its foot. Their hair—so intertwined, it's clear

she's stood like this for some time. His two hands,
stone—one pressed against the wall behind him,
the other covering his beard and mouth.
He can't sculpt, can't speak though he must yearn to,

her mouth right by his ear. Viewed from the back,
the muse could be getting inside his mind.
Here in front, there's no such hint. At some point
she'll have to untangle herself, climb down

from his lap and leave. There's no other way
this sculptor can ever work again.

THE MATH OF IT

Friday Harbor, WA

What's the math
that makes a ferry's wake mirror throat grooves on a whale—

shallow, long
striations across this inlet's silvered surface—

that ferry four
hundred forty feet in length, three and a quarter

thousand tons,
ferry that can carry two hundred cars, two thousand

travelers coming,
going? What's the harbor's length and depth, the ferry's speed

that a floating mass
can be so balletic in its glide toward the dock?

Twenty minutes
late, this morning's 7:40. Only two weeks here

and their winter schedule—
every two or so hours one arrives and within

thirty minutes,
it's backing out to reverse itself beyond this

harbor, continue
ferrying—has plied its cadence within my body.

Or more likely
an expectation of cadence. Ferries coming,

going. The equation
of what opens with what closes. A freighted load,

displaced water.
The balance of what I carry, harbors I must leave.

IN THIS HABITABLE DESERT

the Sierra Cabreras—
repeating pale, sandy hills—
unwind their way to the sea
in unending, sharp-etched lines.
In this country of the saint
I read before arriving—
John of the Cross, his *Dark Night
of the Soul*—both the massive
and the minuscule echo
his urgings, repeated urgings
to find my way to my own
interior. As just now
when I took off my dusty
sneakers and socks, a snail's shell
fell to the dark brown rug. I
could not miss it. John writing
for his brother monks, of course,
but four hundred years later,
I reading as writer, how
else read his call to journey
with nothing, go inside that
dark night, involuted
as a snail's spiraled chamber,
sprawling as a mountain range.
Go in at the land's pace, pace
of what dwells here. John teaching

not to run away from what
would carry me where I could
not go on my own, where I
could not even imagine.

THE MUSIC MAN

Right here in River City, the Music Man warns,
underlining each word of his lyrics in red,
each emphasis as alarming as a Rothko slash
across a canvas or the shadow of a red-tailed hawk
kiting above a field, that shadow as real a presence
to any rodent below as the raptor himself.
Right here, he sings and a rash of dread spreads over the city.
If only inspiration could arrive that readily,
a band rising on cue to Harold Hill's punctuating
arms, brass-edged notes reaching inside every parlor,
spare room, and pool hall. Sure there are techniques for making noise
you can teach a band or a group of writers. Today, though,

my subject's inspiration, endangered as the Right Whale,
but oh, so surely there when it's there and rising, that rising
a rising in you. Surprising, too, as the flash of red
on a wing when the bird you thought just black and ordinary
lifts from a thicket of marsh reeds. I want the writers I teach
(eight women from the North Shore. We meet in Rockport, in one's
dining room overlooking the harbor, its fierce seawall
of reassuring granite slabs from the local quarry.
Each meeting I send them on a rudderless journey beyond
such a wall. I should be lighting candles, praying rosaries
for exposing each one to such waiting risks and ruins.
I think of Renoir at the end of his life, insisting

his favorite brush be tied to his hand. I think of Rembrandt
recognizing that the crosshatches he etched and etched on one plate
took him places sketching never could)—I want my writers
to find flashes of red right here in the everyday grays,
red as when a flicker turns its head, rat-a-tat-tat-tat-tat,
seventy-six trombones' worth of conviction rushing in behind
every line thereafter. And awe. Awe as from the Rose Window
at Chartres, how it held me mid-aisle, the way the red fox
religiously traveling through my back yard at dawn still can
as I draw open the bedroom drapes. Even if some lines
aren't clear to the group, let these women find ropes and pulleys
to lift their work off the ragged page, Roman candles sparking

long after the final word. Or if revision's where the real
writing occurs as Mark Doty says, then give them strong rakes
to remove the dry and the dull. There's something to be said
for Professor Hill's "think system," how the imagination
invents out of nothing, sure as reindeer pull sleighs full of toys
or Redon's dabs of paint really are tissue-thin flowers.
Sure as band jackets, the color of dried blood, can morph
to the-British-are-coming-red coats. Some think saints' relics
cure ravaging disease, depression. Well, so, too, the here-and-now:
out my living room window, despite the hundredth inch of snow,
breath of a male cardinal across the yard. In his later years,
Yeats fled Dublin each winter for Rapallo. Nothing stopped him

from writing. He knew inspiration—the imagination
on fire—favors the ready, inspiration a kind
of resurrection, all of us the same dry and dull
twenty-six letters till the stone's rolled away, the familiar
voice calling us forth. You know you're ordinary as a robin
and yet, each spring what does the first one do? A roomful
of Raphaels, a Rubens altarpiece could not loosen
winter's hold more swiftly, such promise in that rust-red breast.

Right here in River City, though the first song says, *You gotta know the territory*. Rats! It took me years of teaching to learn I can't inspire anyone. Nor are there rolling pin or player piano gimmicks to "make nice" of the wreck

on any page. Writing's a frontier you ride out to alone—that end-of-the-line *right here*, Professor Hill just outside, *a hundred and ten cornets right behind*.

WHERE

Where the *Acushnet* met the *Lima* near the equator.
Where Herman Melville, a green hand aboard the *Acushnet,*
met William Henry Chase, a young teen aboard the *Lima,*
Chase the son of the first mate on the *Essex,* rammed and sunk
by a sperm whale before William Henry was born. Where
father and crew survived three months in whaleboats, eating
those who died. Where the younger Chase loaned the future writer
his father's book, *Narrative of the Wreck of the Whaleship*
Essex, book the son had brought with him to sea. Where Melville
read "this wondrous story upon the landless sea & close
to the very latitude of the shipwreck"—this where
where converged in the waters of the Pacific an ending,
a beginning. Where Melville first sighted *Moby Dick.*

THE DESIGN

Then there was the day He was seized
by the need for the tiger lily. Orange,
but not subdued. Not pumpkin or peach.
More aflame, though not oriole nor that rust
of red heads, red fox. Closer to koi
in those mysterious ponds. Yet not.

Red-orange for tiger lilies alone.
Each nodding flower, petals swept back
in a calligraphy of curls and curves,
trumpeting six stamens. That perennial,
native to China where they eat its bulb.

Not: tiger lilies would be nice to have.
No, their necessity. If we'd never
seen one, how insatiable our craving.
The places we'd never go otherwise.

THREE

IT WILL NEVER GET ANY BETTER

Four years they did not come out of their cottages,
she says, women the new Ireland lured from Africa.
Every day, wind and rain, if not from one side,
then the other, if not downpours, at least mist
and some of that heavy, no telling when in the day

the clouds would open, one storm passed through, another
always on the way, keeping them in. They were
waiting for weather they knew, not Connemara
skies, perpetual raw gray. Like them, I've had to
learn it will never get any better.

You have to dress in layers, two at least, then rain gear
over that. Otherwise you won't ever go out.
Maybe a bit of an exaggeration,
the four years she said. But I'm here four days now
and it's not gotten any better. Rain-dark clouds

keep moving across. This morning it was snowing.
Yesterday I got caught in hail. I'd started
in sun, though I was dressed for hail. And hail it did
on my way back, the turn in these skies that swift,
that dramatic. Mind you, daffodils are in bloom

along every path. I walk the lanes, curving
and narrow, around this place. Maybe a car
or two will pass in the hour I'm out. I've learned
they won't slow, won't yield right of way. I've had to
go down into the ditch to let them pass.

A SUNDAY SKY IN RAIN

Tyrone Guthrie Centre, County Monaghan

Here's the sky I've been given this Sunday morning,
monotonous in its dirty white cloud cover,
singular, darkening rain lines above the hills.
Wait. Wash that. Add more black to the gray, more light below.

And now a mist is creeping this way from those far hills,
coming as close as the lake below where it settles blue-
gray among the thickets and pines. Their needle-sharp shapes
soften, drift in and out of view. I look down, write
a long line and in that space, a breeze has pushed in.
Even under the thickest of clouds, the wide lake
shimmers. Drops of rain prick the surface. Then it goes
glassy. Puffy clouds appear just above the distant hills.
Rain leaks from the lowest ones. Which way is it turning—
the sky I've been given this Sunday morning?

Late morning now, the slightest dimming of light,
there are too many subtle shifts to capture. The hills
are swallowed. The gray line of clouds grows heavier.
Rain falls for ten minutes. When it lifts, two swans—
white mounds asleep—are in the picture. What subtle shifts?
Surely not the half dozen black cows come out of the pines
across the lake. And suddenly the former sky's back,
monotonous in its dirty white cloud cover.

But not for long. The sun, the sky are trying, blue
on this side of the lake while rain clouds beyond
the hills grow darker. Close in, the puffy clouds build,
their domes enormous. Now there's depth, there's near
and far in the sky. Darker lines yet spider throughout.
Afternoon's arrived. The sun's faint glare has traveled
one end of my windows to the other. Brushes
are still busy, trying out deeper shades of gray.
Shadows lengthen across the lawn running down
to the lake's edge. Which will win out: the fragile blue sky
or the darkening rain lines above the hills?

Evening's coming. It hasn't rained for a few hours,
though it might have. All day the lamp on my desk
has been burning. Who'd have thought an overcast sky
would be so hard to pin down? Before today I'd have said
nothing changes here. Earlier the resident hares
were racing each other over the soggy lawn,
getting their multiplying act going. Flashback
to the bull on a cow's back on the way here.
Anything is always easier than the task
at hand. So back to the sky, Moira. Add more black
to the gray as the light begins its slow dying.

THE INSISTENCE OF YELLOW

After "Thirteen Ways of Looking at a Blackbird,"
WALLACE STEVENS

How much yellow suffused this morning's gray
wrap of sky. Throughout the day yesterday
rain had held that cover close to itself.
Late November. All month it has rained
or was going to. The stark maples, lost
in meditation, know the rain's involved
in what they know. There's very little I know.
In this early light every bird is black.
The way they can't stay still mirrors the way
I meditate. How long can you stay with
a stark maple? All November it has rained
or was going to. Rain's involved in what
I know. Nothing has depth. An ancient mountain
weights my ribs. Still, narrow bands of yellow
open my heart's good eye. It looks around.

ADVENT

Testing the ice, ritual these days on the pond
Here before me. Two boys, book bags dropped on the stone bench,
Edging out, out and then a delivery truck driver

Wanting to check for himself: guys who play hockey
Or now a woman whose child must—all gingerly
Right foot, left, slip-sliding away from land's edge,
Desiring to be held again, ice to hold,

Over the ice to push off, one foot, then the other,
Flying head on into the wind. Lone skater now

Gliding out toward the pond's deepest part, or into his
Own deep thought. Out there, only the clothes on his back,
Drawn forward by grace, its sweep—right skate unto left.

THIS LOT

Our destiny depends upon a place
so why not this one.

"VIZCAYA," SPENCER REECE

And once again the frontier between earth—
or at least my backyard slice of it—and fire
is about to be closed. Distance closed. Earth
lying in wait as I do here at my desk. Earth,
bedrock of gravity, its own dome of air,
such a happy union, each in its place. Earth,
eons of experience: dawn always arrives. Earth,
my companion as we both sit by this pond
though at the moment darkness still owns the pond.
The pond's just faintly there. I want it to be there. Earth,
stately as a heron, now wading toward the first light.
Indiscriminate in what it will first bless—light

some mornings, it seems, choosing itself, light
as it swims forward to meet the edge of the earth,
reflecting itself back by degrees. Light
luxuriating in beginning again. Light
oozing into a warm gray, *Here comes the sun,* fired
through with shots of mauve and pink. Move over, Night. Light
coming over the small hill so that at this hour it
first finds the tops of trees, moves down along the air
between the branches below, greening that air.
Only at this hour, this low angle, does the light
brush the white breasts of the geese on my pond,
geese turned toward the warmth. Distance closing on this pond

as the sun coats the bowl of land down to the pond,
the remains of a glacial receding. Light,
picking up speed, now travels the length of the pond
in no time. Few cars yet on the road between my pond
and the one beyond. How everything on this earth
longs to be filled. Nothing but runoff feeds this pond.
And rain. We want the rains long and slow on this pond.
Or a deep snow cover, gradual thaw—slow fire
that prepares the way for spring's arrival. Fired
clay is what we are: vessels, pitchers, bowls. A pond,
empty but for what runs off, falls. Reflecting air
in the spaces between the lily pads. Just air

at some mile above, becoming sky. Only air,
then sky, then space: frontiers above this pond
I've faced every day for thirty-five years. Air,
the one avenue I know to infinity. And light.
Swallowing long, deep lungfuls of spring's green air,
I dream I can leap as fish do from these waters. Air—
however briefly—holding me high and free. Air
filling the holes in me, my work. Yet to break from earth's
gravitational pull, a rocket needs thrust. Earth
owns each body. This place owns me. I've walked on air,
though. I swear, I've walked on air here, charged with the fire
that is cardinal or osprey as it dives, on fire.

At my desk I'm at such a remove, the world on fire
with war upon war. I sit here empty as air
too many hours a week. Men set themselves on fire
during Viet Nam. I came of age during that fire.
We've learned nothing. From an upper room on this pond,
behind locked doors, I praise a red fox, maples on fire.
Or give thanks. They could be the same prayer. Fire,
with its ever-shifting truth of beauty and light.
Each of those cars, a destination. I long for light
every morning of the year, for my gray lines to fire

and lift, close the distance between heaven and earth.
The pond, though, always wants me to come back to earth.

This lot, my destiny. No better source on earth
for inspiration, what showed itself as tongues of fire
above the Apostles' heads at Pentecost. Even air,
that lover of distance, sidles up to me on this pond,
whispers in the wind: *It's coming for you—that light.*

THE HABITS OF RAILS

Birding 101, he begins and I'm ready
to be attentive though thinking just now of my class,
women working on poems, the one I've assigned
for this Tuesday—an irregular refrain. Sudden
repetition, not where you'd expect it. He's saying,

Nothing sudden. No sudden pointing or raising
your binoculars. Should you see one, describe where
in terms of the face of a clock. Mid-May evening
at the edge of the Lynnfield Marsh. I've joined a group
looking for Virginia rails, bird I've never even
heard of, let alone seen. What am I looking for?

Surprise us, I tell my students. "Hen-shaped marsh bird,"
says the guidebook when I get back home, "flight brief
and reluctant, secretive habits and mysterious
voices, bodies laterally compressed—hence 'thin
as a rail.'" These house-high grasses and reeds, ideal
for cover. We're following abandoned rail tracks

into the marsh. "Usually calls are the best clues
to their presence but by patiently watching
at the edges"....When we come to an opening,
the leader plays a tape of its call. Listening there
on a railroad tie, I'd swear a train's chugging toward us,
but no rail's flushed out. "Why do I write all this?"

and Yeats answered himself, "That I may learn at last
to keep to my own in every situation in life."
In the thick of things one woman calls, *Marsh wren, three
o'clock*, and a choreography of binoculars
trains on the spot. I fix where they're facing, but again
I'm too late. *Good eye, Elizabeth*. The leader knows her

by name. An hour and a half gone by. One Wilson's
warbler, tell-tale sign, its black cap. Now I'm trying
to find ten o'clock. I feel like a heavy bird.
Our leader reminds us it's the rail we're after,
moves us along. I want my students doing the same
assignment, finding out how the irregular

can delight. Someone spies *a marsh wren, eleven-fifty*,
but at the edge of my right eye—movement
on the other side of the tracks. There before me,
my binoculars bring it in close—a yellow bird,
its yellow could not have been more primary,
scarlet markings, as if someone's fingernails, dipped

in paint, had been drawn down its chest. I don't call out.
I keep to myself. I'm supposed to be looking for rails.
I know it's not the assignment, a student says
from time to time—and now I can say with her—*but*
one evening at twilight in a marsh in Lynnfield
the yellowest joy went shuddering right through me.

WHY TODAY?

.

The year's two cygnets, everything they need,
right here on this pond: splash of water lilies
over the surface, plants that cling to their stems
below, parents hovering nearby. And besides,
it's late September, they're nearly full grown.
What's there to fear? So, indulge me. Ponder
with me *what* they feel *where* in their bodies
that might make them, maybe later today, lift,
lower, lift again, for the first time not stop
lifting those wings. I mean, they're not fledglings,
food no longer being ferried to them
high in some nest, hunger what drives them over
the edge so that they fall into the flap
of their wings, they fly. No, I want to know
why today these two might keep pounding air,
ponderous wings, at first just a pulse throbbing,
then a hurry in that pounding, a thrust
raising them, taking them right out of this pond.

PSALM 8

The birds of the air, the fish of the sea
and whatever swims the paths of the seas
now before this ferry, its front wall of glass,
Sitka spruce all along the shore and inward
into green-black forests. Left side and right
I search for the hunched profiles of eagles,
want their eyes mine, penetrating this state's
vast wilderness, missing nothing that moves,
especially one of them in flight, such purpose
in each giant wing flap. Once through the narrows,
I want *whatever swims the paths of the seas,*
spray of a humpback about to surface.
I stop breathing to wait for the salute
of its tail as it slides back under. Oh,
do that again. Of *whatever swims,*
I fasten onto what rises, here now
breaching porpoises, four of them arching
over the arctic depths from which they rose.
I ache to follow them below, fathom
such darkness and know—all walls of glass gone—
I, too, am meant to come back up, every time
my body silver and shining, flying
with porpoises through *the paths of the seas.*

LET ME COME BACK IN SEPTEMBER

Tyrone Guthrie Centre, County Monaghan

Let me come back in September when summer's still in the landscape
and autumn's making only the briefest of forays, in at dawn,
then gone till twilight. Nights I will already need a comforter
for my bed, but just a light jacket during the day when I walk
the wooded path out to the lane. The path will be dry, the trees

still leafed out. I long to be walking the lane in September
toward the distant hills, their overlapping rises stretching along
under clear skies. For two weeks, March weather—wind-carried
    rain, at times
horizontal, at times turned to sleet—has kept me tethered here,
those distant hills, far too far when I walk these days, always looking

over my shoulder at the ever-approaching rain-fraught clouds.
I long not to worry how much time I have before they arrive.
In September holly and ivy will twine through the hedges
above the ditches. I won't need this rain gear or waterproof boots.
Let me come back to walk in September in each day's warm hours,

arms and legs in sync with long pulls of breath opening wide my lungs,
pressing me on toward those hills. What lies beyond? Likely more
    of them,
as green and boggy, singular trees stranded atop their rolling crests.
In September the lake will still be brimming with fish. Every hawk
will have its fill. Oh, let me come back. Let me say it was so.

PRAISE SONG

The child is eleven, the third of three brothers
so: fearless and tough. You know, Whatever
they can do....Also, the colorful one,
the dreamer. Last week, wanting blue jays and robins
to breed (he called it *mix together*). *I'd like that,*
he said, looking out toward the woods. This week
he's asking if I've seen the grave, he's nodding
toward their back yard. *I dug a hole out there,*
he says, *to bury the bird I found. A robin,*
he answers me. *I put a stone on top.*
Then it needed a name so I named it Wings.

Wings, what he wrote on the stone. This child,
who is only eleven, naming Death *Wings.*
Already knowing the universe of flight
and loss, this child accepting the offices
given unto us to perform, the ones we find
on the paths we walk. Because he walked
behind their house, because he found a dead bird,
the instinct to minister took over, told him what to do.
Now on my path—so due to chance, so foreordained—
this child who's eleven. This child named Evan.

BENEATH AN IRISH SKY

Having just arrived, I can't say if it were days
of showers or just one storm—maybe no longer
than a fierce hour—left the ditches this slurry
of mud, slick and red-brown. A thick brush has spread
watery clouds, a gradient of black to rain-
gray, blurring in their hurry. These clouds, shrouds
unwinding over hillocks, or rising sky-
filled washes. Are they coming? Going? I worry
I'll be caught without an umbrella so I turn
back to the house, though in my turning, turn
already from my purpose, having just arrived,
here for two weeks to be beneath a sky so vast
I can do nothing but be emptied—or is it
filled?—all my purposeful striding, stopped in its tracks.
When I look back at where I was, there's a cloud
of a profile, its mouth a crescent moon's
open gape. Bright light radiates from behind
its other cheek, no sun visible but no doubt
there. Sunday's Gospel about the Prodigal Son
or, depending how you read it, the Prodigal
Father. No need to walk any farther. Just look up—
north, west, south, east—there's your inheritance.

NOTES

"Widow's Walks." I am grateful to the Nantucket Historical Association Research Library for the materials it made available for me to read.

"Where." Eric Jay Dolin's *Leviathan: The History of Whaling in America* is the source for the story of the *Essex* and the Melville quote.

"The Habits of Rails." The bird book information comes from Roger Tory Peterson's *Eastern Birds* and David Allen Sibley's *The Sibley Guide to Birds*. The Yeats quote is from one of his journal entries as recorded in R. F. Foster's *W. B. Yeats: A Life*, Vol. 1.

ACKNOWLEDGMENTS

I begin by thanking the editors where the following poems appeared, sometimes in earlier versions:

Atlanta Review: "Entering the Cill Rialaig Landscape." First place grand prize winner of the 2016 International Poetry Contest.

Boston College Magazine: "Praise Song"

Christianity and Literature: "Sentence" and "Where"

Crab Orchard Review: "From This Distance," "Let Me Come Back in September," *"The Sculptor and His Muse,"* "Toward"

City of the Big Shoulders: An Anthology of Chicago Poems: "Too Much to Take In"

Green Mountains Review: *"The Music Man"*

Innisfree Poetry Journal: "Widow's Walks"

Nimrod International Journal: "The Math of It," "Psalm 8," "Where There's a History of Famine"

Notre Dame Review: "Advent," "The Design," "Genealogy," "The Habits of Rails," "The Insistence of Yellow." "Genealogy" was reprinted in *Notre Dame Review: The First Ten Years*.

Poet Lore: "It Will Never Get Any Better"

Wild Apples: "This Lot" (originally titled "Muse")

"Beneath an Irish Sky" received Honorable Mention for the Erika Mumford Prize in the 2015 New England Poetry Club contest.

I also thank the following for the time and space they gave me to begin many of these poems:

Cill Rialaig Project, Ballinskelligs, County Kerry, Ireland

Fundación Valparaíso, Mojácar, Spain

Tyrone Guthrie Centre, Annaghmakerrig, County Monaghan, Ireland

Helen Riaboff Whiteley Center, Friday Harbor, WA

I am grateful for permission to include lyrics from *The Music Man* in my poem by that title.

Rock Island
from Meredith Willson's THE MUSIC MAN
By Meredith Willson
(c) 1957, 1958 (Renewed) FRANK MUSIC CORP. and MEREDITH WILLSON MUSIC
All Rights Reserved
Reprinted by Permission of Hal Leonard LLC

Ya Got Trouble
from Meredith Willson's THE MUSIC MAN
By Meredith Willson
(c) 1957, 1958, 1966 (Renewed) FRANK MUSIC CORP. and MEREDITH WILLSON MUSIC
All Rights Reserved
Reprinted by Permission of Hal Leonard LLC

Seventy Six Trombones
from Meredith Willson's THE MUSIC MAN
By Meredith Willson
(c) 1957 (Renewed) FRANK MUSIC CORP. and MEREDITH WILLSON MUSIC
All Rights Reserved
Reprinted by Permission of Hal Leonard LLC

I am grateful for the time and critical attention that Barbara Siegel Carlson, Nancy Hewitt, Dawn Paul, Mary Pinard, Martha Silano, and Myrna Stone gave many of these poems in their various iterations. An earlier version of this collection benefitted significantly from being workshopped in a Colrain Manuscript Conference led by Joan Houlihan and Martha Rhodes. I thank Gregory Wolfe for his attentive and thoughtful editing of my final manuscript. And, as always, my most heartfelt thanks go to my family members and friends who surround me with their abiding support for, and interest in, this work I do.

This book was set in ITC Galliard, designed by Matthew Carter and published in 1978. It is based on the sixteenth-century type created by Robert Granjon. The name Galliard refers to a lively dance of that era and Carter's type has long been admired for both its energy and elegance. It is perhaps best known for its "pelican-beak" italic letter "*g.*"

This book was designed by Shannon Carter, Ian Creeger, and Gregory Wolfe. It was published in hardcover, paperback, and electronic formats by Wipf and Stock Publishers, Eugene, Oregon.